T0386652

ITALIAN
CUSTOM MOTORCYCLES

*The Italian Chop –
Choppers, Cruisers,
Bobbers, Trikes &
Quads*

www.veloce.co.uk

First published in March 2013 by Veloce Publishing Limited, Veloce House, Parkway Farm Business Park, Middle Farm Way, Poundbury, Dorchester, Dorset, DT1 3AR, England.
Fax 01305 250479/e-mail info@veloce.co.uk/web www.veloce.co.uk or www.velocebooks.com.

ISBN: 978-1-845843-94-6 UPC: 6-36847-04394-0

Readers with ideas for automotive books, or books on other transport or related hobby subjects, are invited to write to the editorial director of Veloce Publishing at the above address.
British Library Cataloguing in Publication Data – A catalogue record for this book is available from the British Library.
Typesetting, design and page make-up all by Veloce Publishing Ltd on Apple Mac. Printed in India by Replika Press.

ITALIAN
CUSTOM MOTORCYCLES

The Italian Chop –
Choppers, Cruisers,
Bobbers, Trikes &
Quads

Uli Cloesen

VELOCE

Contents

Foreword

I like motorcycles. In fact, I'm obsessed with them. They've fascinated me since, as a young lad, I saw a Norton Commando overtaking my parents' car on a German motorway. The combination of the power, the sound and the aesthetics of bikes endears them to me.

This book investigates the rich tapestry of Italian custom bikes from around the globe. Note that we're talking 'powered by Italian motorcycle engines' here, not Harley customs or the like built in Italy. Whilst not definitive, the collection does give a flavour of what's out there.

Motorcycles from Italy are primarily associated with the sportsbikes sector, so it's befitting to show that there can be a rather nice other side to them, and there are quite a few Italian beauties around.

I hope you enjoy the amazing bikes in the book as much as I enjoyed bringing it all together. Ride on!

Uli Closen

Introduction

Life would be dull without a dash of individuality, creativity and flair, and this is particularly true when it comes to our two-, three- or four-wheeled modes of transport. There has to be an emotional connection, a feel-good trigger that engages us to build, ride or drive.

So, what exactly do we mean by custom motorcycles? Generally, these can be bobbers, choppers, cruisers, trikes and quads.

Bobber motorcycles were first created by US servicemen returning home after World War II. They wanted bikes more like those they'd seen in Europe; motorcycles with less bulk than the homegrown varieties. A bobber was created by 'bobbing' or shedding weight, particularly by removing the front fender and shortening the rear fender, with the intention of making the bike lighter and faster. The more minimalist ride was perceived to look better than the standard machines. Note: not all countries allow the removal of fenders on bikes.

It wasn't until 1969, when the American road movie *Easy Rider*, starring Peter Fonda, Dennis Hopper and Jack Nicholson appeared, that the term chopper arrived on the scene. Motorcycle enthusiasts once again found a new way to modify their bikes. People started changing the angle of the front fork, reducing the size of the gas tank, and adding ape hanger handlebars to their bikes. To round it off, a thin front wheel and a large rear tire were added to the package.

The main difference between bobber and chopper bikes is that bobbers are usually built around standard frames, while chopper frames are often cut and welded to suit. Bobbers also often lack chromed parts and long forks.

The term 'cruiser' refers to bikes that copy the style of American machines like Harley or Indian. This segment of the motorcycle market is most popular in the United States, and the 'Big Four' bike manufacturers – Honda, Kawasaki, Suzuki and Yamaha – all produce Harley clones for this very important market. Riding a cruiser typically entails a feet-forward riding position with an upright body, and chopper motorcycles are often considered cruisers in this context. The low slung design of this type of bike tends to limit its cornering ability, though.

Italy has a rich history of building three-wheelers, starting in the late 1930s. Firms like Moto Guzzi, Gilera, Moto Morini, Benelli, Bianchi and others all produced 500cc three-wheelers. Because of tax incentives surrounding their use, they were very popular with businesses for carrying goods, and they were faster and more agile than tractors, and had payloads between 300 to 1600kg. Many had mechanical or hydraulically tilting load platforms. In one sense one can see these three-wheelers as the ancestors of the modern Italian trikes of today.

A trike is in essence a three-wheeled motorcycle, carrying its rider and up to two passengers, depending on specifications. If you don't like the idea of riding a bike, but are after the thrill of the acceleration and speed of a motorcycle, with the safety of an added wheel, a trike might be just the thing for you. In many countries you don't have to wear a helmet when riding a trike, because they can be registered like a car.

Quads were first introduced in the 1970s with the Honda US 90, the first all terrain vehicle (ATV). Less expensive to run than a pick-up truck or tractor, smaller and more maneuverable than either one, and with their low-pressure tires which were easy on soft ground, ATVs became essential tools in farming, and even as a means of mobility for the disabled. A new branch of quads is road-oriented, comes with high-performance engines, and some models have chassis more similar to those of cars than motorcycles.

ACKNOWLEDGEMENTS

The author and publisher wish to acknowledge their debt to all who loaned material and photographs for this book. Thank you also to Moto Guzzi Australia. You are welcome to contact us to have your Italian chopper, cruiser, bobber, trike or quad considered for an updated edition of this book in the future.

CHAPTER 1
APRILIA

The company began life as a bicycle manufacturer, and later produced scooters and off-road machines, but has more recently been known for its race-winning sportsbikes. In fact, Aprilia became the most successful motorcycle racing brand in history in 2010, surpassing even MV Agusta, with a record 276 wins in Moto GP and World Superbike championship events.

In 1985, Aprilia began outsourcing engines for some models to the Austrian company Rotax, which also built the Rotax-engined BMW F650 from 1993-1999. Aprilia is now owned by Piaggio, the world's fourth largest motorcycle manufacturer.

In terms of custom bikes, Aprilia started producing the Red Rose 50 and 125cc in 1988, the company's first custom bikes using Rotax two-stroke engines.

Left: The 125cc version.
(Courtesy Motorpresse Germany)

The liquid-cooled, single-cylinder two-stroke engine delivers 27.2bhp at 10,250rpm.

In November 2008, Aprilia unveiled a new concept model called the Mana X at the Milan Motorcycle Show. The bike is based on the semi-automatic Aprilia Mana 850, and styling inspiration seems to come from American flat-trackers. The Mana X uses a motocross seat, stacked projector headlights, and chunky tyres. The exhaust is located underneath the engine, in Buell style, to show off the chunky billet aluminium swingarm. Braking is achieved by wave-style rotors, and Brembo-like radial-mount calipers.

It remains to be seen if Aprilia will enter the custom bike sector.

Aprilia's idea of a fun, stylish, urban bike. The Mana X concept bike was penned by Miguel Galuzzi, who designed the Ducati Monster in 1992. (Courtesy Alessandro P)

At the EICMA in Milan 2008. (Courtesy Jeremy Knight)

The bike features a trellis frame and upside-down forks. (Courtesy Alessandro P)

CHAPTER 2
DUCATI

ucati was founded in 1926 by Adriano, Marcello and Bruno Ducati in Bologna. The company built its first 175cc 'Cruiser' in 1952 – a four-stroke scooter with automatic transmission and electric starter. Best known today for its sports motorcycles with desmodromic valve design, steel tubular trellis frame and the L-twin engine, the company took its first foray into custom cruiser-dom in 1986, when it commissioned bike builder Dallas Baker to produce a prototype using an Cagiva Allazura engine. The factory then created the Indiana Custom, using a 53hp 650 Pantah engine in a box section cradle, with raked forks, teardrop fuel tank, and low seat height.

The engine wasn't ideally suited to the cruiser genre because its wasn't sedate enough, and the Indiana didn't appeal to either Japanese cruiser buyers or to Ducati fans, and failed to sell in sufficient numbers. Production lasted only two years, and 2318 units in total of 350cc/650cc and 750cc variants were sold.

These pictures were taken at the Ducati display tent at the 2010 Indianapolis Moto GP. (Courtesy speedfourjoe)

Fast forward to 2010, when Ducati lifted the veil on its Diavel power cruiser.

EICMA Milan November 2010. (Courtesy Alessandro P)

Ducati's new 1200cc Testastretta L-twin muscle bike is a bold attempt to diversify its model range and to grab a slice of the popular cruiser market. It might well pay off, there are plenty of people who like sports cruisers but don't want a Harley.

Maximum power is stated to be 162hp, dry weight is 207kg, ABS, traction control and adjustable riding modes are promising features. The power-to-weight ratio should make the Diavel a very worthy competitor for Yamaha's VMax or Harley's V-Rod.

Upper left: The trademark trellis frame is retained. (Courtesy Steve Harmon)

Bottom left: The bike is long, low and raked. (Courtesy Steve Harmon)

Below: The 240 section rear tyre. (Courtesy Alessandro P)

LUCA BAR, DESIGNER, WWW.BAR-DESIGN.NET

Before the Ducati Diavel materialized, Luca commented in March 2010 about his D66 concept proposal: "Everything started when some rumors came out about the possibility that Ducati was designing a sport-cruiser bike for the US market. Maybe you have seen something about the Vyper concept of another Italian designer. In my opinion, to enter the US market a sort of Ducati VMax was not the best choice, the bike would have to be something more similar to the HD V-Rod.

The Ducati D66, is aimed, somewhat, at the V-Rod market segment. With the V-Rod aiming at a slightly different and a bit younger demographic than their other big twins, it seems perfectly logical for a Ducati design to look in the V-Rod's direction, perhaps there's a crossover point where both machines would appeal to the same riders. Others have used the Ducati as the basis for choppers and customs so this is certainly within the realm of design possibilities."

The D66 has a 1098 engine, and is fitted with a 240in rear wheel.

The Tricolore version.

TOTTI MOTORI, BOLOGNA, WWW.TOTTIMOTORI.COM

Roberto Totti's Ducati-based custom bike, the Desmodson. The bike was built in 2007, based on a 1000cc Monster. Totti's idea was to create a Japanese-style minimalistic bobber. I think he achieved it rather well.

The Desmodson.

Another angle on the bike.

The Totti bobber.

OBERDAN BEZZI INDUSTRIAL DESIGN, RICCIONE

Many great concepts have come from this designer's pen. The mixture of old scrambler look, mated with the Desmo engine is rather appealing, and is included in the book purely as an act of self indulgence.

Ducati Desmoscrambler 696 design.

Front view of the Ducati Monster quad bike.

A Ducati Monster quad bike parked outside the Misano Race circuit, Rimini, Emilia Romagna, as seen in July 2007.
(Courtesy Michael B Moore)

A rear shot of the quad.

We continue with Ducatis from the United Kingdom. This chopper was spotted in Yorkshire.

Left: This chopper was spotted in 2005 by William Thomas.

Below: The same bike in 2001 at Shaw Lands, Barnsley. It's certainly worth a look! (Courtesy Steve Greaves – www.stevegreaves.com)

ALLMOND CYCLE DESIGN
WWW.ALLMONDCYCLEDESIGN.COM

Roger Allmond's Techno bobber was built in collaboration with Ducati UK, and was influenced by his design studies at Coventry University. Everything on the bobber was handmade bar the radiator and tyres, and it took 10 months to complete. It's a piece of art.

The engine produces around 150hp, and the bike features a trellis frame and a wide rear tyre. (Courtesy Horst Roesler – www.motographer.de, and World Championship of Custom Bike Building – www.amdchampionship.com)

A springer-fork Ducati chopper seen in the early 1980s.
(Courtesy Bob Williams)

This Ducati trike was on show at Arrow Mill on a 'Day out for Ducati Monsters.' (Courtesy Ian Bower)

A Ducati chopper at the Shires Show in 2009. (Courtesy Harry from Wales)

TAFF BAKER'S DUCATI CHOPPER

Taff's story: "One day, whilst sifting through piles of bike bits at Russ Taylor's emporium I came across a wrecked Cagiva Gran Canyon. This bike had a newish Ducati 900SS motor and it seemed a bit rude not to buy it and stick it in the shed.

"Time passed, and, after a holiday, I was diagnosed with cancer. What was needed was a project to take my mind off the prospect of dying. We all have big ideas that we put off and off and off. But let's face it, if not now, then when?

"After about five weeks of recovery, I was bored out of my wits and thought what I need now is to do some welding. A massive spending spree ensued. AC/DC TIG set. A small secondhand lathe and miller, and sundry other bits were shoehorned into a 9 feet x 18 feet garage, and I locked the door behind me.

"First task was to knock up a box section jig. Into this sturdy frame were clamped my first purchases, a spoked Harley sportster wheel at the front, and a Triumph T595 wheel at the back. The engine was mounted on angle iron mounts, to give a nice cool 4.5in ground clearance. A headstock turned up to accept the standard spindle and bearings, and was mounted at a rakish 40 degree angle

"The key to the look of the bike was to build a thin tube frame, which appeared to be somewhat missing at the front end. It was also

The rear wheel is from a Triumph T595.

very important to make the frame higher above the engine than on a conventional Ducati, in order for the vertical cylinder to be clearly seen. The frame was fashioned using a plumber's bender, some heat, and a lot of BFI (brute force and ignorance); tube is 1in diameter, 3mm wall CDS.

"Mating the T595 swingarm with the frame was a major pain, and took three attempts to get a working unit. The shock is a unit from a CBR 600, which was short enough to keep the rear end low, and the length-to-height ratio of the bike is about 1.6:1 (as are lots of other parts of the bike).

"I wanted to create a fork system that I had never seen before, and for this I used 'schedule 30' stainless steel tubes (6mm wall thickness). The lower pivots are turned in 316 stainless and have two roller bearings in each. Pivot arms and clamps are also 316, and suspension provided by good old C90 shocks.

"The front brake carrier is a milled ally plate, and the torque arm is a stainless bar with rose joints. This particular item had to be remade a couple of times due to the original torque arm position allowing too much rotation of the caliper (as with the rear suspension lots of trial and error).

"Slab yokes were milled out of billet on the new milling machine, and the original stem adapted to fit. Now that we had a basic bike structure the next problem was where to put all the fuel-injection gubbins? The original plan was to run the motor with a big 'sod off' Dellorto twin choke, however, I got advised by several guys that this was a non starter due to ... something or other. So gubbins it was, and quite a lot of it, too!

"Under the tank then ... In my original sketches the bike had a small coffin tank and clip-ons; however, by the time we had a 35mm void to house the gubbins, the tank would only hold enough fuel to get to the shops and back. As you can see, the small coffin tank remains, but on top of that are two things: A rounded shell-type thing, and a shark mouth thing as a homage to Chica, the best tank builder money can buy!

"All of this shape was raised using a hammer and dolly in 3mm ally plate, which I annealed with an oxy-propane torch.

"The tank is topped off with a Shaun Barley filler cap, a speedo off eBay, and some copper pipe, just because I love the look of it. As a tank it's a bit weird, but seems to work (and holds 3.5 gallons)

Taff Baker and his beauty.

The chop from the side.

"The rear mudguard is also hand formed. The handlebars and risers were made to suit the position of the tank, and also to be comfortable for long journeys. Master cylinders are taken from a V-Rod, and levers have been made from solid copper bar.

"The foot pegs and foot controls are all made to suit, using ally and stainless, and positioned again with comfort in mind. The exhausts are made from 2.5in food grade stainless pipe. Once all the bits were made we had a marathon polishing session (about two weeks solid). Anyone who has ever polished will know what it's like to come in looking like a coal miner, it gets a bit tedious after day four.

"Paintwork was entrusted to the Mighty Dave and Al of Big Al's Paint Shack, who without much prompting just came up with the goods.

"Soap box time now. Here we have a chopper, light, nimble, bloody fast, nice handling and pretty radical, but above all a MOTORCYCLE. Customs that arrive and depart in vans are NOT MOTORCYCLES they are paperweights.

"Thanks as ever to all the people who helped. It's Sandy for constructive criticism. The Malpass, Toshy, and the marvelous Mr Swaby for assemblage assistance. Last and by no means least the lovely Victoria, for tea and strength.

"I'm also much better now, and thanks for asking."

A close-up of the front suspension.

PETER KOREN'S XR900

"Five years ago I bought an abandoned project based on a 900GTS. The seller intended to make a Hailwood Replica but gave up on it. It was a non-runner due to a rusty tank and no battery. The engine was covered with white fur, and I bought it for spares for my 750GT and 900SS.

"However, on closer inspection it was better than I thought, and after fitting a battery and tank from the GT, plus a gearlever, it fired up second kick, and after a short road test I knew all gears worked, as well as the brakes.

"The bike was too much gone to consider restoration, so what to do with it? It stayed in the garage for a couple of years while I mulled over the idea of a flat-tracker.

"The main elements that distinguish the Harley XR750 are the tank and seat, the curvy high-level exhaust, and the clean front end with spool hub. I had no intention of running without brakes, but by reversing the fork legs and having the calipers behind I improved the look enormously. One weekend while my father was staying, I made a mock-up XR750 tank and seat out of Cellotex, a polyurethane insulation foam that is really fast to work. Dad sat in the sun drawing the tank graphics and my son helped painting.

"I liked the result and decided to proceed with certain parameters: I would try to build it as if it came out of the Ducati factory, which would determine many of the details, and the budget was set at £500 plus tyres and chain. The budget was low because it would always be a bitsa, and also because of fear of failure. I wasn't sure it was going to work and I've seen plenty of modified bevel Ducatis that make me shudder.

"It was quickly obvious that a Harley tank would not fit the Ducati frame, but I bought a replica seat base and handlebars from the USA and made a wooden buck for the tank. I had a sheet of aluminium, made a sand bag, and cut down one of the kids croquet mallets and started bashing. Then I had to learn how to gas weld aluminium, which was tricky, and weld up the bits.

"The XR750 has no side panels, the left side is mostly covered by the exhaust, and the right is covered by a large racing numberplate. The way the frame tubes go on the Ducati, the sides looked a mess so I decided to make the side panels using shapes from the seat unit as a guide, as well as shapes on SS and GT panels. First I had to straighten the kink in the frame tubes that go up from the rear engine mounts because I wanted a slim-waisted look, and the standard frame would push the exhaust too far out. Something still didn't look right, and it took me some time to identify that it was the steering head angle, which was then steepened by five degrees.

"Footrests are GTS butchered and welded, the gear change fabricated in GT style. I abandoned the brake crossover shaft because it interfered with the new position of the left footrest, and made a new brake lever and cable that crosses under the seat.

"I really enjoyed making the exhaust. I had loads of old headers

The Ducati flat-tracker.

It really looks like a factory model.

to cut up, but found I needed a tighter bend under the front cylinder and eventually found a grab handle as used in toilets for the disabled. For the record, I did not steal one!

"The silencers have cut-outs for the rear shock like the Imola high level pipes, so they sit nice and close to the frame. Heat shields were first bent around an old silencer and then drilled. Tail light is a Cateye bicycle lens on a home made alloy housing.

"Next, I fitted a light and made speedo and tacho housings in the style of the Scrambler 'Beer cans.' This also meant I had to compromise on the handlebars and fit switches, which spoils the clean look somewhat, although I ran the wiring through the bars. I gave the seat pan to Earl who did a lovely job cutting the foam and covering it. Got the tank decals cut and printed on vinyl and sprayed the lot with Harley Racing Orange basecoat and 2K clear lacquer (My God, do I hate painting!).

"I didn't like the original plastic ignition housing on the rear bevel and, with my newfound skills, made one from aluminium.

"What's left to do was to wheel it out of the garage, put in some fuel, kick it over a few times with ignition off to get fuel in the cylinders, and it started first kick.

"Brilliant reward after three years, and the cheap far-eastern silencers sound amazing with a really deep thump."

Lee (Grobo) Robinson's home-built Ducati chopper was one of the winners of the Carole Nash Britain's Got Biking Talent Challenge in 2010

"The idea of building a bike especially to suit my tall frame was sealed by seeing the new (at the time) American Chopper series on TV. Eventually, I ended up tracing a side view of a Ducati Monster and modified its dimensions to fit my six foot four inch body. This was it, and I went out to buy a used 1996 M900 Monster. Aftermarket parts

The Ducati Monster chopper took 18 months to build.

The extended fuel tank, seat, tail unit, and 900cc engine are the only Ducati Monster bits: the rest is all handmade.

were sourced from US and German Ducati websites, and eBay provided the carbonfibre, bell-shaped airfilter assembly. I made up some one-off manifolds to hook up the filter with the twin 42mm Mikuni carbs, and to channel the fuel/air mix from the carb to the combustion chamber. The two-into-two, heat-wrapped Dan Dare exhaust system was fabricated in stages with my friend Coxy. Although I have never built a frame before I decided to build a trellis-type chassis for this project. The forks of a Ducati Paso were used to replace the stock legs with ten-inch overstock stanchions. A 17-inch single disc wheel and four-pot Brembo caliper were rescued from a 125cc Cagiva Minto and secured to the frame by 50mm thick aluminium slab yokes machined up by Chopper

The trellis frame is 4in longer than standard, made from 32mm tubing. The MH900e-style swing arm is extended by 6in over standard,

Club member Andy. Coxy made the one-off 70mm diameter stainless fork shrouds, while I fed the braided stainless brake hose inside a long stainless steel hose rather than running a line through the yokes. The handlebars measure a full four feet, and are comprised of two separate bars made from 35mm stainless steel tubing. The rear wheel stems from a 15in magnesium Subaru rally wheel modified with a Ducati 916 hub and a five-stud wheel nut conversion. I built the single-sided swinging arm by using 50mm and 32mm diameter CDS steel tube, secured by a heavy-duty dual bolt clamp. A Ducati 916 shock absorber with a ride height adjuster soaks up the bumps. The original Monster fuel tank has been extended downward at the back to hide electrical components behind a one-off panel covering the underside of the tank, secured by being bolted to the rear cylinder's tappet cover. The Acewell digital mini speedo/rev counter unit at the front of the tank is held by a one-off spring secured shroud. The build cost me about £4500, but that is because I made most of the parts myself."

US-built Ducati customs are next.

DESMO DEVIL PROJECT BY MARK SAVORY OF MOTOCREATIONS.COM

"I like to challenge the norm. Break the rules. Go where no one has gone before! In October 2003 I came up with the radical concept of recreating a Ducati sportsbike as a chopper. I knew this would upset many of the Ducati purists. How dare I take an Italian motorcycle that epitomizes the thrill involved with passion and riding and convert it into a stretched-out cruiser. But the idea of pushing the envelope of acceptability only made the challenge more tempting.

DESMO DEVIL
1995 Ducati 900SS/CR by MotoCreations

Fabricated parts:
  Chromoly frameset
  Triple clamp assembly
  Tubular rearsets
  Tubular GP-style shifter
  BoomTube underengine open exhaust system
  Twin-Tube clutch cover
  Desmo Devil bodywork
  Custom seat
  EuroFlat headlight assembly
  Electrical system
  Tubular chainguard
  Tubular sprocket cover
  Tubular plate holder assembly
  Custom-valved Penske rear shock
  Custom electric fuel pump

Modified Ducati parts:
  Singlesided swingarm conversion
  Ducati 900SS engine w/FCR carbs

Ducati parts utilized:
  996 Front Showa fork assembly
  996 SSS assembly
  996 Brembo brakes
  Two-valve 904cc Ducati engine
  Ducati Monster front fender
  Ducati Monster handlebars
  Ducati gas cap assembly

"Engineering and building the motorcycle were a challenge, as I felt it was essential that the bike have the cornering clearance, suspension, and handling characteristics needed to remind the rider that he/she was part of a motorcycle still connected with the famous Ducati racing traditions. I wanted the framework to be stronger and cleaner in design than the original. I wanted the bike to be lighter than the basis of its origins. I wanted the Desmo Devil to have the heart and soul of a Ducati while also retaining the design language of the Miguel Galuzzi original. And most importantly, I wanted the American statement of stance and profile to be instantly recognizable.

"We built this motorcycle just because we thought it would be cool. By February 2009, this bike appeared in 42 magazines throughout the

This photo was taken by John Sachs on Ducati Island in July 2007 at the US GP, Laguna Seca, California.

world. The last of the Desmo Devils have been created and delivered to customers. At this time, due to the large amount of specialised labour to create – they are no longer part of our regular product offering.

"One day we will build more ... but not yet ..."

13 CHOPPERS OF OCEANSIDE, CALILFORNIA

Matt Zabas' custom bike design philosophy is best described as lightweight, functional, high-performance, custom American-style bikes powered exclusively by Ducati engines.

"When we designed our choppers we wanted to keep a lot of the original Ducati elements, including the basic frame design, and as a result the bikes we build are very performance-capable. They turn very well, with plenty of ground clearance, and benefit from high-performance Brembo brakes, Ohlins or Showa suspension. Aircraft aluminum components and carbonfiber use are also part of the package.

"We're just waiting for the rest of the world to catch up with the idea of a radical custom bike that actually works, that corners, brakes, and goes plenty."

13 Choppers took two of its bikes over to Italy for the World Ducati Week 2004, which won it the custom bike contest. When the CEO of Ducati and the head of design handed over the trophy, it was one of the most memorable accomplishments the company has had. Three of 13 Choppers bikes have been captured here.

This picture was taken by Christian Knuetter Photography in 2008, at the Laguna Seca Ducati stand.

This 13 Chopper was photographed in 2002. (Courtesy Corey Levenson)

A second 13 Chopper at the same Ducati stand. (Courtesy Christian Knuetter)

TreMoto, Taylor Mississippi
WWW.TREMOTO.COM

TreMoto was founded in 2009 by Eddie Smith and Rob McIver. After meeting in the School of Engineering at the University of Mississippi, Eddie and Rob decided to take their senior engineering project to the next level. The TreMoto Monster 620 is the result of two years of bootstrap engineering to achieve the dream of creating a safer, more capable alternative to two-wheeled motorcycles. TreMoto's patent-pending Leaning Vehicle Suspension System can be applied to nearly any style of motorcycle. The company says that in creating a reverse trike with a patented leaning suspension, like the one based on a Ducati Monster 620, TreMoto has found the ultimate way of combining the visceral thrill of riding a motorcycle with added safety and stability desired by riders everywhere.

"The little Monster is more composed on gravel than a KLR or GS, and more confidence-inspiring on the pavement than our Z1000," says Rob McIver, CEO of TreMoto. "It is the best of both worlds, on-and-off road, without the compromises most dual-sport or adventure-touring motorcycles make.

"Having two front wheels is like the auto-balance feature from a Tony Hawk video game. It's sort of like a Piaggio MP3, but replace the 'scooter' with 'Ducati,'" Smith adds.

TreMoto vehicles lean up to 45 degrees, just like a motorcycle, and are controlled completely by the rider; no electronic 'band aids' are required. The company's second prototype, (Kawasaki four-cylinder based) coded 3Z1, competed in 2011 at the 89th Pikes Peak International Hill Climb.

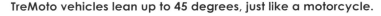

TreMoto vehicles lean up to 45 degrees, just like a motorcycle.

The trike is powered by a 620cc Ducati engine. (Courtesy Jimmy Smith)

TreMoto's patent-pending parallelogram double A-arm front suspension.

LLOYD BROTHERS MOTORSPORT, OHIO
WWW.LLOYDBROTHERSMOTORSPORTS.NET

Although the Lloyd brothers' Ducati is a flat-track race bike, home-built in their barn in Ohio, it deserves to be mentioned in this book simply because of having made history.

Their rider Joe Kopp won the first mile of the 2010 season on this bike, in a sport where from 1994 until 2009 every single race on a track of a half a mile or longer was won on Harley's XR750.

Dave Lloyd: "The frame was designed by our team, and fabricated by VMC Racing Frames. The triple clamps are from Baer Racing, and the forks are Honda F4I. PM wheels, Penske shocks, and Brembro brakes."

At the All Star National Series ½ Mile.

Joe Kopp won the AMA Grand National Mile in Prescott Arizona on May 1, 2010.

Rider Larry Pegram on the track.

LEIPERS FORK CHOPPERS, TENNESSEE

Eric Jackson tells the story:

"We bought a wrecked Monster 900 just to get the engine then began ripping the old carcass to pieces, it was then you can truly appreciate how well the bike was built by the factory. We started by mounting the engine to a couple of straight frame rails, and then I began building back to the rear and then to the front so I could completely control the proportions of how the odd shape engine nestled in the frame, and keep an even gap all the way around it and its miles of wiring that had to be hidden. We thought about converting it to a carb setup, but it runs so smooth with the fuel-injection. This project took six months, and it was the most challenging build we ever tackled, but the challenge is what made it worth tackling, as anyone can put a custom V-twin together, but it takes a different vision and determination to tackle the king of all bikes; Ducati. We have been to many shows where Harley enthusiasts discount it as a metric dud, that is until it fires up and drowns out all surrounding bikes through its straight custom exhaust. We love it, and it is truly a one-of-a-kind, and unreal to ride as the power is amazing. Once you hit 55mph it feels topped out, and then you ring the throttle and it surges to 100 before you know what happened and feels like an afterburner kicked in.

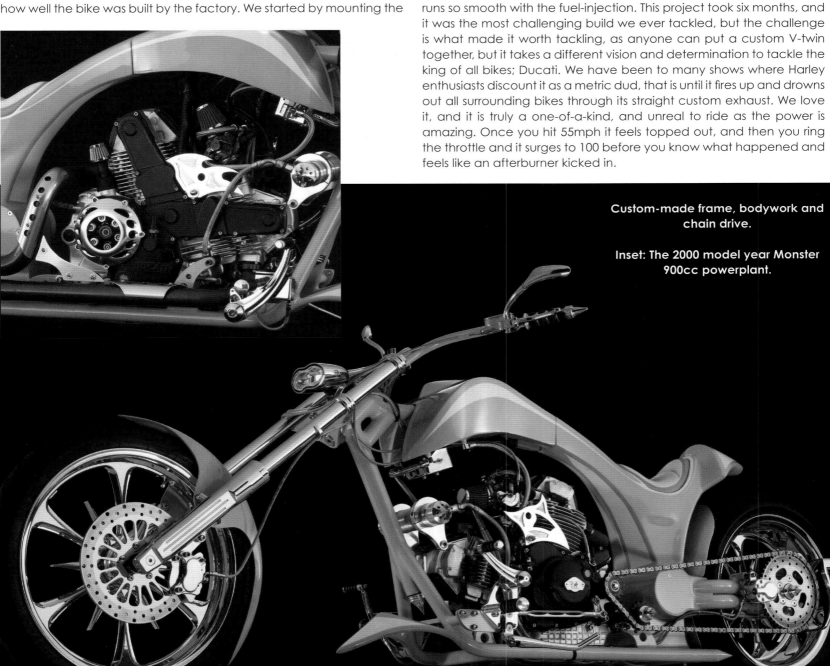

Custom-made frame, bodywork and chain drive.

Inset: The 2000 model year Monster 900cc powerplant.

"Specification? 45-degree fork rake; 250 rear tire; custom-machined oil cooler and rear hub; custom Leipers Fork Chopper frame; single-sided swing arm; rotor (disc) brake system; full custom sheetmetal; GPS/speedometer; fuel-injected; basically everything custom."

Dunlop 250 rear tyre.

FLIGHT CYCLES, RESEDA, CALIFORNIA
WWW.FLIGHTCYCLES.COM
The Coup D'etat

Stuart explains: "I had an idea for a SuperSport swing-armed, Monster-framed chopper in my head for about six years. I did some initial sketches years ago and lost them in my move to the LA area. Suffice to say, the final version you see here is vastly different to my sketches.

"The frame which eventually became the Coup D'etat was from an engine donor that a friend had purchased on the internet. He wanted the engine and wiring and sold me the frame for a song. The rear half had been run over by a car in an accident (rider was okay), and was badly twisted up, but the front half survived quite well. So, I cut the rear stub off and hung the front stub in the rafters of the shop until I could sort out the rest of the build in my head.

"The engine in the bike is a M900, which was also from a wrecked bike. This mill has the heads (750 cams and valves) so it is less desirable for all-out performance. The smaller valve train actually suits this bike just fine, as torque is the order of the day.

"Rear suspension duties are handled by a 2000 SuperSport steel swing-arm from a wrecked bike, and the same adjustable Sachs shock, too. The upper frame of the swing-arm was cut off during the lowering of the seat, and a trellis-style support was built up on the left side of the arm. The rear wheel is off a Honda Shadow VLX from a local salvage yard. I was looking for a wheel with a 17mm axle so as to avoid changing bearings out and making spacers. It looked a bit fat on the bike initially but it did have a 160 tire on it.

"The front end is off of a Suzuki Savage. I took the entire front-end to make certain I would only have to adapt one thing, ie the steering head bearings. I wanted a front-end with a simple lower fork leg, big spoked wheel, single-disc brake, and a nice set of triples. The Suzuki delivered on all counts. I had to have a spacer lathed up for the upper bearing, and ended up using a Kawasaki lower steering bearing with a custom machined outer race. After adapting the bearings, it all bolted right in without any issues other than the steering stops were different.

"As the project progressed it was clear that the bike wanted to become something different. More Bonneville, less boulevard. More flat-track, less drag-strip. More low and lean, less tall and boisterous. So I took the front fork springs out of the sliders and rolled it outside for a look-see. From that moment, low and lean was the order of the build. The mini-Apes went into the dumpster and a pair of drag-bars were donated by my friend Dave M. The rear shock was repositioned from the standard SuperSport location to a lower point on the left side of the bike to allow for the rear seat to position itself directly behind the vertical head. Originally, the build was to be powered by a 750 engine, so the frame tubing above the vertical head was positioned as such. Somewhere along the way I thought about what makes a true hot-rod bike: a big engine. I test fitted the 900 engine several times before realizing that it was too tall as it sat; so, out came the grinder. I ground the frame a bit, and the head a lot. It is a snug fit,

Coup D'etat. (Courtesy Jules Cisek – photo.popmonkey.com)

The rear shock has 1in of suspension travel, which translates to 2in of suspension travel at the wheel.

The bobber has a Honda Shadow VLX rear wheel.

but you may be able to squeeze a piece of paper between the head and the frame.

"After deciding on the lowering, I had to decide on the finishing. Primer black? Gold? Red? How was it all going to turn out? As always, the project evolved into what it wanted. Primer (looking) black and red with chrome and polished bits. The color scheme for the bike was lifted out of the folder of dream cars in my head. A black primered Ford coupe with red wheels.

"The electrics and wiring on the bike needed to have an 'old' feel to them. To accomplish this, I hid as much of the wiring and electronics as possible, and dressed up those that couldn't be hidden. The battery sits on the swing-arm, covering up the main power relay and the starter solenoid. A special bracket below the engine holds the voltage regulator and the charging fuse. The fusebox and ignition system are located on a special bracket in the tunnel of the 1.7 gallon fuel tank. Lastly, the horn takes up residence on a bracket off the front of the engine, down by the starter.

"To add to the 'old' feel of the bike, I chose wiring from a tractor restoration supply house. It is modern wire, but with the cloth covering over it. A lot of people comment on how different and cool it is. Personally, it was just one of those touches that needed to be done. A 1952 Ford Ranch Wagon ignition switch was purchased and wired into the loom. The circuit powers the ignition and lighting, while the 'START' position turns on the starter. A YTZ7S battery was fitted because of its small size.

"Construction took four months initially, and another three months after its debut."

Ride and final impressions

"The bike rides great and performs almost all tasks quite well. The bike is a touch short on stopping power, but a larger caliper is being looked into as an option to solve that woe. The footrests are a bit too low, but then again so is the rest of the bike. The 140 rear tire is a bit too narrow for drag-race style starts or wet weather starts, but for most duties sufficient to hold the high-torque 900 in check. It's not your average Ducati, but it does get the same amount of looks from people; just a different crowd of people that's all."

Stuart would like to thank the following businesses/individuals for their help with his project:
Dave M and Richard R – West Coast Cylinder Heads, Reseda CA
Jim G – Granger Classic Auto Body, Reseda CA
Cycle Stop, Los Angeles CA
Pyramid Powdercoating, Sunland CA
Derek – Distinctive Metal Polishing, Chatsworth CA
Lee – Lee W Pedersen Tractor Restoration Supply, NY
Gil G
Zak G

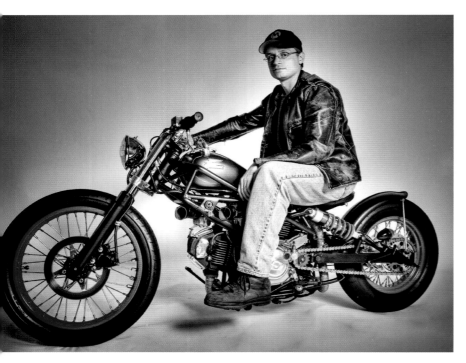

Stuart on Coup D'etat bobber.

SPECIFICATIONS

1999 Ducati Monster frame with serious tail-chop and the neck raked out to 36 degrees

1998 Ducati Monster 900 engine (est 60hp)

HD wrinkle black paint and exposed fins

Polished side covers, belt covers, cam-end covers, and valve access covers

2000 Ducati SuperSport swing-arm flipped upside-down (to lower the rear), and the upper support removed

1988 Honda Shadow VLX rear wheel, hoop powder-coated Baron Red with polished hub and stainless spokes and nipples

1988 Suzuki Savage front end complete with fork sliders cut to lower the front

1988 Suzuki Savage front wheel, hoop powder-coated Baron Red with polished hub and stainless spokes and nipples

Tires: Continental Blitz. Rear: 140/90/15, Front: 100/90/19

Exhaust: Home-built duals with fender washer baffles and VW Beetle tips, all wrapped up in header wrap

Intake: 2x Mikuni 34mm round-slide carbs on custom manifolds with custom velocity stacks

Unknown origin 1.7 gallon fuel tank painted Benelli dark-grey with red pinstriping

Universal aluminum rear H-D fender painted Benelli dark-grey with red pinstriping

Vespa/universal scooter kill switch and horn button

Universal headlight with Hi beam switch drilled into the top of the bucket (now with Loris Capirossi signature!)

Marsh Instruments pressure gauge screwed into right side engine cover to monitor oil pressure

1954 GMC tail-light on custom bracket off of swing-arm

KULICK ENTERPRISES INC
WWW.KULICKENTERPRISES.COM
Ultra Duc

Robert Kulick and his team's concept motorcycle, codenamed 021, came into being as an intern project in Michigan. The prototype was developed to show what they could do. The bike is street legal, and the chassis was custom-built by Kulick Enterprises. It was a project to develop a lightweight bike targeting smaller riders.

The project is taking shape. (Courtesy Kulick Enterprises)

The bike is based on a Ducati 748. (Courtesy duccutters.com)

RICKY GONZALES, WWW.LUCKY13GRAPHICS.COM

Ricky: "This bike either has people wanting to kill me or praise me. This started because of my love for Ducati motorcycles. I came across a wrecked 916 and it started from there. I didn't want to make a Harley lookalike, and I know the paint is cruiser-like, but if you look closely at the bike you will see I kept and added many Ducati and race inspired parts. Like Olins R&T forks, Penske rear shock, Speedymoto pressure plate and slave cylinder, milled clutch engine side cover, billet oil filter, Billet belt cover, Moto Master front rotors and a Gaffer rear rotor, Motocyco Grenade reservoir, Beringer billet brake and clutch master cylinders, MadDuc rear caliper mount. Wheels are from a MH900E. I kept the Ducati rear single-sided swing arm. I didn't put a huge tire on the back; it's a 190. It's got Discacciati six-piston front calipers, and the stock Brembo caliper in the rear. The seat is leather with a crocodile center insert by Hot Rod Interiors. The original 916 engine had internal problems so I swapped in a 944 engine from a 2000 Ducati ST2. This is not a Monster frame. The frame is a one-off custom. It's not a stock frame that was bent or stretched. It's made from 1.25in diameter chromoly tube. The only thing stock on the frame is the neck. The fuel tank was split and widened to fit all the electronics under it. The exhaust is a double shotgun design. The frame, fuel tank, triple trees, handlebars, rear sets and exhaust were done by Mark Savory at Moto Creations. I took the stock 916 tail and modified it and integrated the brake lights and blinkers in the tail. I also fabricated the lower fairing. It is made from round tube with a 0.040 steel skin. It has a Gemo topgun front fender. It has a Motogadget speedo and tach. There are a lot of Billet add-ons to this bike that I made, like the spike bolts, frame plugs, gas cap and exhaust tips. The kickstand has a duck foot base that I got from Bill Johnston at Duccutters. The bike only weights 305lb and moves out pretty good. The paint was done by Peter Weber custom. The guys at Racecity Powersports in Mooresville NC helped me with final assembly. There are so many more mods, I could go on forever. As far as I know according to Mark Savory at Moto Creations this is the last Hyper Devil going to be made. I'm proud to own it."

The Hyper Devil.

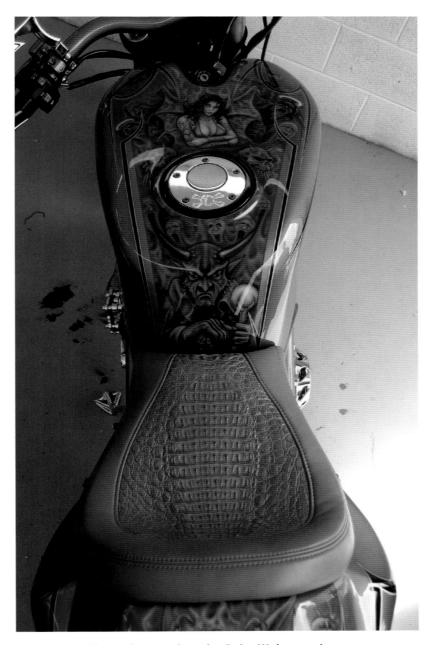

**The Scrambler at a motorbike convention in Holland.
(Courtesy Deirdre)**

and designing street quads, such as the Ducati Monster and Ducati 916 quad shown here.

The paint was done by Peter Weber custom.

We're now moving on to Ducatis from Germany. The picture above right shows a JvB Ducati scrambler.

BKE Motorraeder, Bloensdorf
WWW.MOTORRAD-KLOSE.DE

The strength of Bernhard Klose's workshop is in working on projects such as improving sports bikes, offering parts for off-road sidechairs,

The Ducati Monster-based quad.

The Monster quad front suspension.

MONSTER QUAD
Motor Ducati M900 or M1100
170kmh with M900 motor and 75bhp
Frame Ducati S4R (other frames are possible). Additional brackets welded on using TIG-Argon
Parts for frame and subframe, etc, from CrNi 18.8 steel with front stabiliser
Tie-rods from high-strength aluminum
Wheel adjustment: The swingarm is adjustable, via an eccentric aluminium adjuster
High-strength steering element (aluminium Alcan F 50)
Radial brakes front, Brembo rear
Showa shock absorbers, Ducati 1098 front
Raiker shocks rear
13in rims; front 8.5in with 190/50/13 Dunlop racing tyres; rear 13in with 225/50/13 Dunlop racing tyres

916 QUAD
Differences are
Max speed with 916 S4R motor and 125bhp; 200kmh
Ducati 996 frame with no changes, all quad parts only bolted on
Rear frame from aluminium
Engine options from 851 to Testastretta 1198 all possible
Shock absorbers: Paoli fully adjustable

The quad from the rear.

The 916 quad.

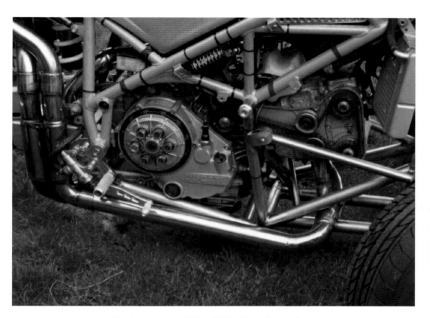

A close-up of the 916 Quad engine.

This drag bike ran 6.6 sec over an ⅛ mile at the Roadrunner festival.

Quad radiator and front cowl setup.

This racer is aimed at running under 10 seconds over a ¼ mile.

Now a brief window into the world of drag racing Ducatis.

Christian Schyma's green racing Duc was specially built for the Roadrunners-Festival (roadrunners-paradise.de)

The red racer is based on the 1098 Duc engine. It hasn't done any race duty yet, and is still being worked on.

WIRTHWEIN MOTOREN, RIMBACH
WWW.WIRTHWEIN-MOTOREN.DE

Dieter Hartmann-Wirthwein presented at the 2010 Intermot in Cologne his V8-powered Ducati Elenore project. It features a custom-built V8 engine with 868cc, all of it fitting into a Ducati 900 frame. This engine would surely look pretty good in a custom bike. Dieter's story:

"My interest in motorcycles began at the age of 12 when I saw two US soldiers starting a BSA 650 on my way to school. The sound of the BSA engine really impressed me. I started riding in 1973, aged 16, on a Maico MD 50. The next bike was a Yamaha DS7, followed by a 350cc bike on the race circuit in 1980. A Ducati 900SS came along in 1983, which I rode until my bike accident in 2002. Since then I am dependent on a wheelchair.

My first large work was converting a Bultaco 350 into a four-stroke. I registered this bike in 1991. In 2005 I made a four-valve head for a BMW R50S. Next, I wanted to build a completely new engine. I constructed a four-cylinder engine for a Honda Dax on its existing housing. My son Fabian contributed much to it, and rode the bike with much joy afterwards. In 2007 I entertained

Looks like a production engine ...

the idea to transform a two-cylinder Ducati into an eight-cylinder bike, now, however, directly with a short-stroke crankshaft. Work started at the beginning of 2008 on the Elenore V8 project. The presentation of the V8 project at the Intermot in Cologne was made in cooperation with Stuttgart University. The engine was put together for the Cologne fair. I have yet to make the beltdrive and re-machine the pistons.

Engine: air-cooled, eight-cylinder, four-stroke
Bore x stroke: 56mm x 44mm
Compression ratio: 11:1
Displacement: 868cc
Output: 60kW (80bhp)
Valve arrangement: two valves per cylinder. Exhaust 27mm 27°. Inlet 23mm 33°
Fueling: Four 28mm flat-slide carburetors
Valve operation: Single cambelt
Crankshaft: Patented connecting rod

The V8 engine fits into a Ducati 900SS rolling chassis.

... very clever engineering indeed.

Dieter and support team at the
Intermot 2010.

Rounding up this look at the world of Ducati customs are two more bikes, one from France, the other from Russia.

Opposite: It looks like a factory machine.

NICOLAS PETIT, DESIGNER
PETIT-MOTORCYCLE-CREATION

Nicholas' three-wheeler concept 2K3 is based on the Ducati Desmosedici RR, and is looking rather nice.

A side-view sketch.

The trike in traditional Ducati colours.

YuriShifCustom, Minsk Belarus
WWW.SHIFCUSTOM.COM

Yuri: "The start was made by a friend, Vlad Sazonov, when he came out with a proposal to do something with a good old Ducati Monster S4 from the year 2000. He wanted it to look like a low-rider, or even some kind of chopper, black in colour, and decorated with skulls.

"The original idea changed during the process of implementing it all. Frankly speaking, there was little left from our customer's idea as well as from the donor motorcycle; its engine, gearbox and some minor bits. But as a result we produced a unique white machine named Duster (a combination of Ducati and Monster), which has really created dust.

"The bike won Best Streetfighter at Custombike 2009, and Italians liked it so much that it won Best of Show at the Verona Moto Bike Expo 2010."

All pictures by Horst Roesler (www.motographer.de).

A well deserved show winner.

DUSTER
Builder: Yuri Shif Custom (YSC)
Year: 2009
Motor: 1000cc Ducati Monster
Transmission: Ducati, six-speed
Frame: YSC
Front fork: Showa, modified by YSC
Swingarm: YSC
Wheels front : 23/4in YSC
Wheels rear: 21/9in YSC
Tire front: Avon 130/60x23
Tire rear: Metzeler 260/35x21
Brakes: YSC perimeter brakes, with GMA (front) and Brembo (rear) calipers
Paint: YSC
Additional info: Tank, handlebars, headlight, controls, seat, exhaust system, etc. YSC

YSC perimeter brakes, with GMA (front) and Brembo (rear) calipers.

The exposed engine is from a 1000cc Ducati Monster.

CHAPTER 3

FANTIC MOTOR

Fantic Motor was founded in 1968 by Dr Mario Agrati and Henry Keppel-Hesselink in Brianza Lecco Barzago. The company produced and exported enduro motorcycles, mini-bikes, and go-karts. Nowadays, Fantic manufactures dual-sport and motard (supermoto) bikes.

Between 1972 and 1977, 16-year-olds in the United Kingdom could ride a moped – defined as a 50cc motorcycle equipped with pedals by which it was capable of being propelled. In 1972, Fantic and other European and Japanese manufacturers began exporting bikes to the UK market, all with some kind of pedal arrangement to take advantage of this 'sixteener' law. Some of these bikes were capable of about 50mph, and were hugely popular. The 50cc Fantic chopper was born, as was the Fantic Tourismo Internazionale model. Both gained popularity quickly. Fantic also enjoyed success in the 1980s in the trials world championships, and had wins at the Scottish Six Days Trial.

The Fantic 50 chopper. (Courtesy S Broberg; www.dogdragons.com)

What a seat backrest!

Note the pedal arrangement.

The engine runs on a Dellorto carburetor.

London, 1978. (Courtesy Tony Cants)

The flower-power tank motive.

CHAPTER 4
GILERA

ilera was founded in 1909 by Giuseppe Gilera in Milan, and over the years earned itself an impressive racing history. Gilera's inline four-cylinder racing engine technology was taken up by MV Agusta in the 1960s, and later by the Japanese. In 1969, Gilera joined the Piaggio Group, which re-launched the brand by focusing on the production of medium and medium-small motorcycles. From 1993, the company focused on the development of sport scooters.

Gilera also built three-wheelers in the 1940s, in line with other Italian manufacturers of the era.

In comparison to this historic three-wheeler is the modern 2007 Gilera Fuoco three-wheeler/scooter.

A rare Gilera three-wheeler, the Motocarro Gilera Mercurio from 1944, with 500cc and 20bhp, but no hydraulic tilt load platform. (Courtesy www.italo-classics.at)

The Fuoco's Gilera 493cc single cylinder four stroke engine produces 41bhp ...
... top speed is 142kph/88mph. (Courtesy Mad Joker)

In the fifties, Gilera decided to establish a factory in Argentina, hence the marque has had many followers there ever since, be it new machinery or classics from the brand. Today, some classics are used for grass roots custom projects. Presented is a window into the '70s Gilera custom scene.

JUSTO SANCHEZ

Justo: "Gileras were popular motorcycles in Argentina, coming in four models in 150cc, 200cc, 215 and 300cc.

"I modified this 1979 Gilera 215cc for a motorcycle expo. I removed the seat, shock absorbers, gas tank and the handlebars to start with. The new seat was manufactured from a metal plate and rubber foam. The gas tank was sourced from an old Puma military bike, and the handlebars are from a motocross bike. The rims and covers are bought, hence not original. If you want to make a chopper you don't need much, only your desire, some cutting tools, and something to weld with.

The gas tank is from a 40-year-old Puma military bike.

Justo's chop all painted up.

SEBASTIÁN PERALES, CHUBUT, PATAGONIA

Sebastián's custom is based on a Gilera Gran Turismo 200cc single-cylinder from 1974, which his dad bought back in 1978. Since then, they changed the piston and removed the old stator and replaced it with an electronic item. Around 2006, his dad gave him the bike and Sebastián built a frame for it.

Sebastián: "I started with the rear suspension, but decided to remove the suspension and make it rigid. I built the wheels, bought the rims, spokes, nipples, street wheels, etc. The front shock absorber came from a Kawasaki Z750. I changed the angle on the frame, so that the front shock would have more inclination. I also chromed the exhaust and the rear fender, which is also handmade.

"I only saved the engine, the fuel tank, and the rear hub from the Gilera; the rest is either homebuilt or purchased."

The 200cc engine is from a Gilera Gran Turismo.

The brief was 'long and low.'

Rear view of the low rider.

The front fork is from a Kawasaki Z750.

ARIEL MUCHIUT'S BOBBER

Ariel said that the building of this custom was very economical, yet still practical and efficient.

Work in progress: front suspension is from an MTV bicycle.

Almost finished, the bobber is based on a Gilera 200cc.

The dimensions are identical to those of the original machine.

PABLO TECCE'S GILERA CUSTOM

Brand Gilera
Model: Macho 200
Year of manufacture: 1978
Engine type: Single cylinder, four-stroke, air-cooled
Power: 14bhp
Maximum power at: 7000rpm
Maximum speed: 65mph
Gearbox: four-speed pedal-shift, left side, one up, three down
Compression ratio: 7:1
Fuel consumption: 85mpg
Carburettor: Dell'Orto UB 22 BS, with bellmouth
Fuel tank capacity: 2.2 gallons
Rear tire: Metzeler 110\80 18 M\C 58H
Front tire: Kings Tire 2.75-18

**A very tidy custom.
(Courtesy Pablo (Poio) Calvo)**

Engine close-up.

Front view.

Pablo and his mount.

LEA LUJAN'S CHOPPER

The custom is based on a 1976 Gilera 200cc.

The classic fat rear tyre.

The heart of the matter.

Extended forks.

Some of Gilera's new offerings in Argentina's bike market are aimed at the custom lover. One example is the Gilera YL275. The bike is powered by a two-cylinder, four-stroke, 270.5cc engine, delivering 12kW/9000rpm and 110kph/68mph. (Courtesy Paula Verónica Vuono)

Gilera also offers a road-oriented quad – the Kodiac 250 Motard. It features a water-cooled, 233cc, single-cylinder, four-stroke engine, and is equipped with hydraulic disc brakes. (Courtesy Paula Verónica Vuono)

LASTLY, A GILERA CUSTOM FROM EUROPE

Jean Marie Maurel from France modified a Gilera Coguar 125 from 2000 (above) into the black custom he envisaged (right).

The back of the original bike was cut off; the air filter is from a Volvo motorboat, while the raised handlebars, the headlight and the tail-light are all homemade.

CHAPTER 5
LAVERDA

Laverda was founded in 1873 in Breganze as a producer of farm machinery. By 1949, however, the company had ventured into motorcycle production. The brand is most known for its sporting 750cc twins from the late 1960s and, later, its 1000cc triples. By the 1980s, the company was in financial trouble, and some attempts were made to introduce new models, amongst them a prototype cruiser named the Hidalgo.

Laverda GS 125 Toledo. (Courtesy Laverda Museum Holland)

The Laverda Hidalgo.

The bike featured a 668cc twin-cylinder engine, and was introduced in the autum of 1989 at the EICMA in Milan. There wasn't much interest from the public, so the Hidalgo never entered production.

Laverda's 125cc class also featured some cruiser variants, one powered by a two-stroke engine from Zundapp, and another, the Toledo, with Laverda's own water-cooled engine.

The Toledo was a development from the LB 125 Custom of 1983, and has the styling of the Hidalgo prototype.

Laverda changed hands several times, and was finally absorbed by Piaggio in 2004, whereupon the Laverda name was finally put to rest.

SPECIFICATION: ONE CYLINDER, TWO-STROKE
Displacement: 123.6cc
Bore x stroke: 54 x 54mm
Max horsepower: 20/8600rpm
Max speed: 130kph/81mph
Year: 1989

ROBERT GRUBER'S LAVERDA TRIPLE CHOPPER, AUSTRIA

Robert's motorcycle career began with three cylinders, though of English origin. When his wild years were over, and with children to tend to, his desire for a bike to 'glide' with grew stronger. He kept dreaming about a home-built chopper with a Triumph engine, but his friend Hirschi, a sworn-in Laverda apostle, convinced him to build a chopper with a Laverda three-cylinder engine – considered a more exotic and durable choice than British motors.

Robert: "I therefore bought a 1000cc engine (year 1975, number 2903), and Hirschi overhauled it. I then ordered a frame from Sweden. Once it arrived, it had to be converted to allow the Laverda triple engine to fit. The fork, including 19in front wheel, was donated by a Harley. After little success with a Harley brake assembly, we decided to use Japanese parts. Using the rear axle of a 1000cc Kawasaki, we bought a 17in rim and fitted it with new spokes.

Parts like the tank and the lighting system were bought-in items, the exhaust system and the side covers were homemade. Without Hirschi and Jim this project would have probably never succeeded! The first test runs with the Laverda chopper were exciting, since it was uncertain how the chassis (wheelbase 1870mm) would behave. The bike proved stable when running straight up to over 200kph/124mph, there was enough ground clearance when cornering, and only slight instability in fast long corners with rough surface.

The engine has been running problem-free since registering the bike in 1992, and hasn't been opened up since. My thanks go to Hirschi (engine, electricals) and Jim (master welder).

Robert's rare Laverda chopper.

Close-up: the classic Laverda triple engine in all its glory.

The fork, including the 19in front wheel, was donated by a Harley.

A Laverda 750 Twin custom from Italy. (Courtesy Giorgio Scialino)

The engine for this French conversion originates from a 1973 Laverda SF750. These engines look very similar to the Honda CB77 engine. The chopper has a clean frontal look due to the absence of a front downtube.

This trike was photographed by Rob Bradbury at Slater's Laverda Day, 21 September 2008. It was a meeting held by the former UK Laverda importer Richard Slater for all Laverda owners. He still sells Laverda spares at his shop in Collington, near Bromyard, Worcestershire.

The trike is owned by Peter Burton. The conversion can be removed and the bike returned to standard. Peter worked hard to make sure he used existing mounting points on the Laverda triple's frame.

Very nice work indeed, including independent rear suspension.

This rare Laverda 75 Trike is one of two prototypes from 1950, and no longer in existence. The engine was a single-cylinder four-stroke, with a bore of 46mm, and capacity of 74cm^3. It produced 3hp at 5200rpm, via a three-speed gearbox. (Courtesy Jörg 'Giorgio' Strehler)

CHAPTER 6
MOTO GUZZI

Moto Guzzi, established in 1921 in Mandello del Lario, is the oldest European manufacturer in continuous motorcycle production. Very successful in Grand Prix racing during the 1930s and 1950s, the company then had a period of mixed successes and ownership changes and is now part of the Piaggio group.

Moto Guzzi was the first to develop a wind tunnel for bike testing, and the first to bring out an eight-cylinder engine. The company is also renowned for its model continuity, leading to a strong brand loyalty from its customer base. Its 500cc Falcone model was produced from 1950 to 1976, and the original V7 from 1966 evolved into today's 1200cc models.

Moto Guzzi's first attempt at creating factory cruisers was with its 350cc V35 and 500cc V50 Custom models in 1982, joined by the 650cc V65 in 1983.

Originally planned for 1999, the Ippogrifo model.

The V65 C from 1984 with touring accessories.

Typical design elements were a larger, narrower front wheel, and a smaller, wider rear wheel, not to forget the stepped seat typical of cruisers of the era. A more chopper-styled V35 and V65 were introduced in 1986, renamed as the Florida.

In 1989, the Nevada continued the custom style, which was supposed to be superseded in 1999 by the newly-styled Ippogrifo 750cc.

A company restructure in 1998 resulted in the Ippogrifo project being axed, and the Nevada model was continued.

The 2011 750cc Nevada Anniversario model reminds one of the Harley Sportster Nightster with its two-tone paint job.

The Moto Guzzi Nevada Classic.

The Moto Guzzi Nevada Anniversario.

One can argue whether Moto Guzzi's very successful California range (including its entry level models Jackal and Stone) are cruisers or tourers, but all are excellent bases for customizing.

It doesn't take much to change the California.

Zane Lester's California custom project, New Zealand.

Moto Guzzi started building its very nice Griso 1100cc concept bike in 2006 (perhaps best described as a power cruiser).

The 1200cc 2010 Griso 8V.

The Bellagio 940cc cruiser followed in 2007; again, a very capable machine.

The Bellagio, Nevada and California models were made available in matt black from 2010 onwards, labeled as the Aquila Nera range.

Guzzi's Aquila Nera range.
(Courtesy Moto Guzzi Australia)

The Bellagio Aquila Nera.

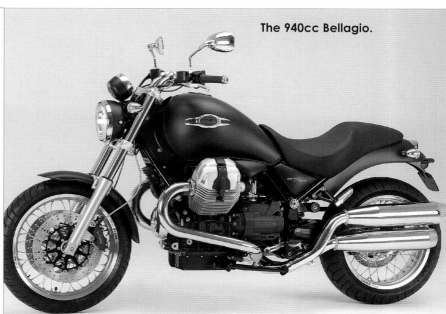

The 940cc Bellagio.

It's time to delve into the world of Moto Guzzi customs. First up are modified Guzzis up to 650cc.

This picture was taken at the Moto Guzzi factory in Mandello del Lario at the Giornata Mondiale Guzzi 2005, an event which takes place bi-annually, attended by up to 10,000 Guzzi riders from around the globe. Naturally, Italy accounts for most of the riders, followed by Germany. This Falcone won first prize for Guzzi customs in the single-cylinder category. The owner/builder is unknown.
(Courtesy Urs Witschi)

This Argentinian-built chopper (owner Lucas Medina) uses a rare 1958 Moto Guzzi Lodola 175cc overhead cam, four-stroke, single-cylinder engine, available in sizes from 175 to 235cc. (Courtesy Manillar)

This Falcone-based chopper has interesting features, such as front leaf spring suspension, rear plunger suspension, and modern disk brakes. The photo was taken in 2010 in Hajos, Hungary.
(Courtesy Huligan)

Smallblock Guzzi V-twins also lend themselves to customization. This Airkult Guzzi chopper was photographed at a 2006 bike show in Italy. (Courtesy harleyvillage.it)

Marco Hansemann's Falcone chopper with a Dell'Orto carburetor under the fuel tank. The bike was photographed at the Bremen Italo Club meeting 2001. (Courtesy motalia.de)

Smallblock custom Guzzi V35, owned by Andrea Cattelan, Venice ...

THE MOTO-BEAM, A GUZZI/SUNBEAM HYBRID FROM THE UK

... it features a custom exhaust and seat tail unit.

Another very nice small block Guzzi custom, courtesy of animaguzzista.com

The Moto-Beam. Proud owner Paul with his Guzzi V50-engined Sunbeam special.

Paul Stabler tells the story: "The roots of the Moto-Beam lay in my first visit to a Sunbeam rally. It was there that I was introduced to John Davies. John is a fine engineer, and his Sunbeam Special was my first beam ride; okay, it was not a true beam, but I liked the way it was not snubbed like in some clubs.

"I still had no intention of a build, and continued turning up to rallys on all sorts of modern Japanese classics, as these were what I ride and had ridden all my biking life.

"The bug, though, finally bit, and I thought of building a special inspired by John's constant tinkering with the beam. The bobber idea was from a Sunbeam I saw many moons ago featuring S7 rear and S8 front.

"I was looking for an engine that could be used but had not been used in a beam before. It had to have style, be an air-cooled bike engine and not a big cc, but I had no idea what would fit let alone just which one from the many engines that lurk at autojumbles.

"I bought a frame, despite the fact it was deadly rusty in all the strength areas, and continued my search.

"The six months I had this frame I acquired many other beam bits and bobs, and during one expedition I found what the donor engine should be. It was in a Moto Guzzi V50, parked up by a fence. The frame now had a use, and measurements where taken and plots plotted; and yes it fitted ... just!

"I was as pleased as punch when I discovered I would not have

"At this point John and I were discussing projects, and, as mine was going nowhere in a hurry, and John was nearing the end of the swinging arm Sunbeam, he suggested, I accepted, and things started to progress.

"There is a long, long list of modifications, but please be aware no beam was harmed in the creation of Moto-Beam. No frame modifications, just cosmetic enhancements for my riding style.

"John has engineered nearly all of the Moto-Beam, but he has listened to my needs on the bike's looks and direction. Between both of us, with help from my dad and other beamers, we have created what I hope is an acceptable contribution to the fraternity of beam family of friends."

The frame came from a Sunbeam S8.

four reverse gears, and that the engine would not exceed the 500cc original Sunbeam.

"After all that excitement things slowed down but I did get a frame with logbook from John that was surplus to his requirements.

"During the next three and a half years I was making promises at rallies that the day would come, but I lacked enthusiasm. I did obtain many more parts, including a roughed-out adaptor plate from John (in which my dad machined the holes and bores in the correct positions), and a V50 bottom end, but time passed.

"So, I now had a Guzzi bottom end and a Sunbeam gearbox, and they fitted into a Sunbeam frame. I had just about all the bits to build, but sadly not a complete engine. Thankfully, eBay came to the rescue and a reconditioned engine was purchased at a very good price.

John Davies, engineer extraordinaire, on the Moto-Beam.

The last of the Guzzi smallblock customs is Raul Pederzini's black bobber from Italy. The bike is based on a Guzzi NTX 650 from 1992, with changes to the frame, suspension, tank, handlebars, etc.

Paul's smallblock Guzzi stripdown in full swing.

A close-up of the exhaust system.

The bobber is taking shape.

The finished product.

Next, three examples of vintage Moto Guzzi 500cc three-wheelers/load carriers (courtesy of www.italo-classics.at). They are perhaps the ancestors of the modern Guzzi trikes presented throughout this chapter.

The Moto Guzzi Ercole from 1949, without a hydraulic tilt platform. Starting is by kickstart only.

Opposite, top left: This Moto Guzzi Ercole from 1965 has 19.5bhp, electric start and a hydraulic tilt load platform. These models were built up to 1979. The factory traditionally painted them in grey, but a lot of restorers prefer to paint them in red to align them more with classic Guzzi road bike colours.

Opposite, top right: The Motocarro Guzzi Unificato, built primarily for the Italian military, dates from 1944, has 18bhp, chain drive and a reduction gearbox.

The bigblock Guzzi custom section is divided into countries of origin. First up are customs from Italy.

Officine Rossopuro (formerly Firestarter Garage) www.officinerossopuro.it, opened in Pescara in 1998. It was the first business of its kind in Abruzzo, being a workshop as well as a shop selling accessories and clothing for custom bikes.

Filippo Barbacane built his first important bike for the 1998 Padova Bike Expo, and has won prices at the annual event ever since. He's focusing on customizing Guzzi bikes in all guises out of pure passion. Filippo has also done work with Ghezzi & Brian on award-winning Guzzi sportsbikes.

In 2003, Filippo started working on a board tracker project, which he named Bellerofonte, after Bellerophon the Greek character who killed the mythical Chimera. The build took only twenty days to complete,

At the Padova bike expo, Italy.

The Bellerofonte upfront. (Courtesy Alberto Sala)

A close-up of the front section.

The Bellerofonte in its long and low glory.

and the bike won first place as the most original and extravagant bike to the 2003 Expo in Padova. (Bellerofonte pictures by Alberto Sala, animaguzzista.com).

This is a mighty rear wheel for a Moto Guzzi.

RossoPuro took six months to build, and won first prize at the 2004 Padova bike expo.

The Ottanta 1000 was built over three months in 2008.

The Guzzi Motard concept bike is powered by the 142bhp, liquid-cooled, 1420cc, big bore engine developed by Giovanni Mariani and Giuseppe Ghezzi from Millepercento near Milan.

This custom is based on a Guzzi SP1000 engine.

The engine is the 1420cc Big Bore from Millepercento; the frame is from a Griso 1100 Guzzi.

TECHNICAL DATA:
Year of construction: 2003
Engine: 1982 Moto Guzzi 1000 SP1
Filters: K&N
Pipes: 1930 Moto Guzzi 500W
Cardan shaft: BMW318 auto
Frame: Homemade chromoly
Fork: Donnie Smith 36in modified. 40 degree rake
Gas tank: Mustang 8l modified
Seat: Front Le Pera, rear homemade
Front fender: Harley softail modified
Rear fender: Benelli modified
Front wheel: Moto Guzzi V7 with 2.15x21in Harley rim
Rear wheel: Moto Guzzi V7 with 4.25x16in Harley rim
Tyres: 3.00-21 / 5.00-16 Continental
Handlebar: mini apehanger with Italjet controls
Footpegs: front homemade, rear Aprilia
Head light: Zodiac
Rear light: Gilera

GUZZI BAIO CHOPPERSERVICE, APIRO
WWW.GUZZIBAIO.COM

Guzzibaio Chopperservice started in 2008 in Apiro, a small mountain village in the middle of Italy. Its primary activity is restoring and customizing old motorcycles, mainly Italian engines. It specialises in Moto Guzzi singles, twins and four-cylinder bikes, and can also build rigid chromoly frames, girder and springer forks, using modern CAD 3D programs.

Andrea's next project is building a rigid Moto Guzzi Nuovo Falcone with 650cc supercharged engine.

This springer fork chopper is based on the Guzzi SP1000.

BEPY MOTO SERVICE, BRUINO
WWW.BEPYMOTOSERVICE.IT

Bepy worked as a freelance mechanic before he started his workshop in 1993 in Bruino (Turin). He loves modifying Harleys or Japanese bikes into choppers/customs, but has a special fondness for working on Moto Guzzis.

The 1090cc Electric Violet was built in 2002/3. Based on an 850T5, it took nine months to build, and won best in show at Biker Fest Daniele's (Udine) 2003, Italy.

The Tribals EV was created in 2006, based around a 1090cc engine. This custom took ten months to build, and won several prizes in Italy in 2007/8.

Bepy's 2008 bike Red Gep is meant to be a symbiosis between old style choppers of the 1970s, and modern technology. It won first prize at the Chopper Bike Expo Show 2009 Padua Italy.

TOTTI MOTORI, BOLOGNA, WWW.TOTTIMOTORI.COM

Roberto Totti is one of Italy's most prolific custom bike builders. This Moto Guzzi creation is rather special. Based on an 850 California, it was constructed in 2006 with the aim of building a bobber, while at the same time remembering the Guzzi Norge from 1928.

Roberto Totti's Guzzi Sport 7 Limited.

Motor assembly in the old style frame.

Front view of the V7 Special.

Moto Guzzi Bobber Red Devil

This bobber stems from Bari in Southern Italy. The California model on which it's based was lowered by six centimeters, achieved by changing the rear section, an extra six degrees of rake in stretched forks, and changing the wheels.

Parts came from a Honda CB750, the wheel rims are from a Harley, and the shock absorbers and a rear wheel brake components were from a Kawasaki GPZ. The 15-litre fuel tank, side panels, exhaust and the rear fender were handmade. Seat height is 690mm. Owner: Guiseppe Coppola.

The 1000cc bobber runs with an Alfa Romeo 75 carburetor. (Courtesy Giorgio Scialino)

The inspiration for the hand shifter came from an Guzzi Superalce from the 1950s. (Courtesy Giorgio Scialino)

Guzzi bobber The Wacky Racer

Luca Marinucci named his bobber after the animated US television series.

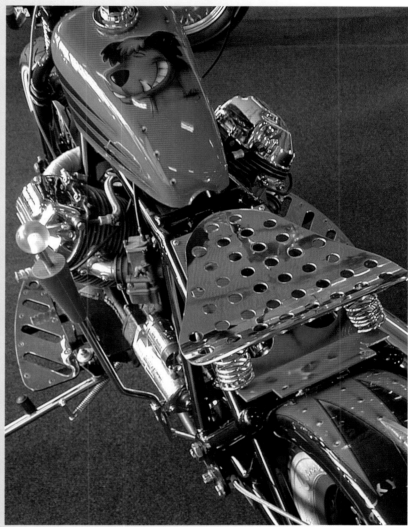

Top left: Supertrapp lookalike exhausts. (Courtesy Alberto Sala)

Top right: The dog face on the fuel tank represents Muttley, one of the protagonists of *Wacky Races*.

Left: The springer fork is from a Harley VLA.

This grey Guzzi chopper (located in Germany but owner unknown) has a re-welded frame, with its shock absorbers placed at a steeper angle. It also has a wider rear tyre than stock. The speedometer and controls are mounted behind the extra-high valve covers (which also emphasise the cylinders). The bike was photographed at the Italo meeting Kiel, Germany in 2005. (Courtesy motalia.de)

MANDELLO – CYCLES, BREMERVOERDE
WWW.MANDELLO-CYCLES.DE

Ingo Pape and his team are custom bike builders specialising in Moto Guzzis. They are also authorized retailers of the brand.

Three bikes from their stable are presented here, starting with the black Easy Rider Peter F, inspired by the 1969 road movie starring Peter Fonda. The motto of this project was 'Back to the Roots.'

The wheels are Morat spoke items.

The rear swingarm is an original Moto Guzzi California III item.

Front and rear mudguards are custom-made of stainless steel. The tank is from a California 1100.

The Dragster was built for a customer who wanted a mix of dragster and low-rider. It uses a Le Mans Mk4 engine integrated into a 1974 T3 chassis, with a 7-oriented steering head.

The swingarm came from a 2002 California, and the modified fuel tank is from an 1100 Sport model.

This version comes with a sprung seat.

A Strada special in red.

Three Strada specials ready to go.

Next up is a Guzzi at home in Bavaria. This bobber, named '1921,' is based on a heavily-modified California model, and was built by a now defunct Munich Moto Guzzi shop.

A very nicely-executed bobber, again showing the versatility of the Guzzi concept. (Courtesy Tom Kohues Photography)

A few images of the New Zealander, a Moto Guzzi custom built by Achim Kindermann in Germany some time ago. Photos are courtesy of www.motalia.de.

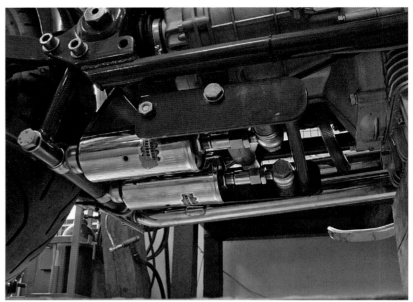

The bike features a two-into-two exhaust system on the left side, and the shock absorbers are mounted under the gearbox. The swingarm and suspension were made by KMS. A fat 200 tyre was the aim of the exercise.

Moto Spezial in South Germany built a Guzzi custom named 'Bassa Lunga.' Here are some images for the record.

The Bassa Lunga (long and low) was based on a 1100 California, had a weight of 198kg, and a seat height of 670mm. The Guzzi engraved exhausts and Fournales shocks are a nice touch.

Maik Evert built this lovely Guzzi bobber. His shop (www.mve-cycles.com) deals with classic motorcycle parts and the in-house production of accessories. He also restores and customises classic European and American bikes.

Maik: "The bobber is based on an 850cc Guzzi engine. The carburetors are of the Dell'Orto VHBT 30 type. The cables run in the modified powder-coated California frame. Exhausts are trumpet style; the fork is original and Koni shocks are used at the rear. The wheels are Borrani high shoulder rims, aluminium polished 3.00 x18; VA spokes, brass nipples. Tires are Cocker Firestone Champion Deluxe 4.00x18. The taillight housing is homemade, and the Hawker battery is under the transmission. Indicators are bullseye type. The modified 12-litre tank is from a Honda CB250. Many parts are copper/brass plated or high grade steel. Other surfaces are pearl radiated or polished, no chrome. Many parts, like the tank, lamp, rear fender, battery, saddle, are fastened by wing nuts, hence can be removed without tools."

The bike features copper/brass-plated items, as well as wooden parts. The speedo, from a Jawa and the oil pressure units are fitted into the tank. Very fine craftsmanship indeed.

The Guzzi custom from Estonia. The Renard design was inspired by the beauty of 1930s-1940s motorcycles – Killinger & Freund (1938), Moto Major 350 (1949), and the BMW R7 Prototype (1934/35), which was also the source of the girder front suspension. (Courtesy www.renardmotorcycles.com)

The Raven custom. Jeff Gundlach always wanted to design and build a motorbike. He wanted to build something unique, powerful, light, functional and with a classic look. This is the result. (Courtesy www.raven-moto.com – Frank J Bott Photography)

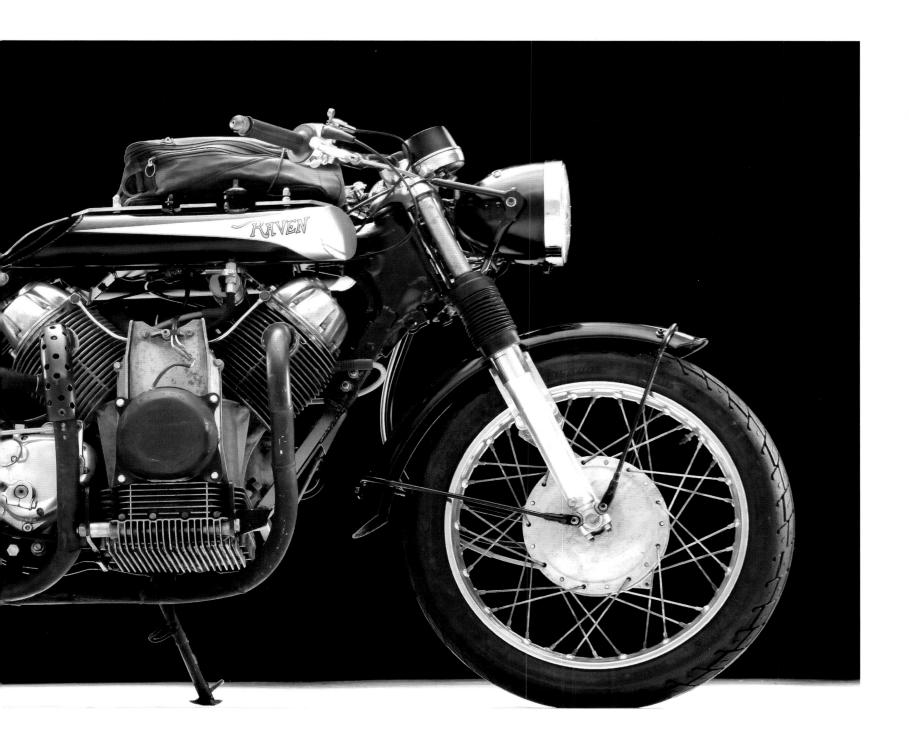

MONACO CYCLE SALES FRANKLIN, PENNSYLVANIA
WWW.MONACOCUSTOMGUZZI.COM

Johnny J tells about his custom: "The bike has won 38 trophies and was judged by Arlen Ness, Dave Perewitz and Dan Hoffman, beating out high-end choppers from different manufacturers. It also took first place at the IMS in Cleveland in Jan 08, from 12 hand-picked customs.

"It was originally a new 2002 Guzzi Stone, except for the bottom frame rails, drive system, and about eight inches of stock frame. I fabricated it from there up, and made extensive mods to the fuel tank – being a FI bike with a lot of components to hide, I used the area under the tank to hide some of them, hence the external air cleaners."

HD wide glide front forks
Sun rims with Bucannan custom spokes (Johnny J)
Modified Le Pera seat (Johnny J)
Avon 150x16 rear (Johnny J)
Avon 110x18 front (Johnny J)
Chrome by Chrome Masters
Rocker Box Xtension (Johnny J, Joe Kenney)
Custom risers (Johnny J, Joe Kenney)
Paint (Johnny J)
Forward controls (Mid USA)
Engine Moto Guzzi (Johnny J)
Mods N/A
Lights (Mid USA)

Johnny J's Stoned Crazy Guzzi custom has won 38 trophies.

Cool Moto Guzzi bobber at the 38th annual LA sidecar rally.
(Courtesy Tim Kuglin – motozania.com)

Seen at the IMOC rally, the largest and oldest Italian motorcycle
meet in the USA. (Courtesy Steven J Cote)

Left and below: This Guzzi springer fork chopper was photographed
in 2007 by Rand Gartman. (Courtesy Aaron Dewar)

WIDOWMAKER CUSTOM DESIGN & REPAIR, ROUGEMONT, NC, WWW.WIDOWMAKERCDR.COM
The Guzzi bob/chop

Hank Thibodeau has had his shop for seven years, specializing in building the unusual. He likes to work with things others do not, and does things with them others would not. He's built everything, from the Guzzi shown here, to a GL1000 Goldwing, and high-end billet and chrome choppers.

Hank says about the build: "As for the bike, it is a 1972 Eldorado 850. I cut the back subframe off, fabricated another and fitted it with Harley Sportster fender struts and covers, and a Fat Bob rear fender. The tank is from a 2000 model HD Softtail.

"The front end is a wide glide front end for a '84-'99 Harley Softtail. The front wheel is a custom-laced 19in H-D wheel with a wide glide hub and dual disc H-D floating rotors and calipers. I made the forward controls, bars, side panels, battery tray, intake, exhaust, and voltage regulator mount. I also made the seat and footpegs, which have 18 golf shoe spikes in each peg.

"The clutch cable is a Harley item. The controls on the bars are Arlen Ness Rad 2 controls for a Harley. The frame, front end, bars, headlight and miscellaneous controls and brackets have been powder-coated satin black, the tins are gloss, and the wheels are ox-blood red. The wiring harness is a one-off done by me. The switch controls, hi/lo beam, starter button, turn signal switch and starter button are all located in the lower backbone gusset below the gas tank."

The starting point was a 1972 Eldorado 850 ...

Photographed at the annual Western Washington All British field meet in Bellevue, Washington in July 2009. (Courtesy Chris Halstead)

GUZZI CUSTOMS FROM THE UNITED KINGDOM
The Pembleton Guzzi by Alan Walker

Alan Pembleton's is the only custom four-wheeled car in this book, but included since it is powered by a Guzzi motorcycle engine.

Alan reports: "Having built and thoroughly enjoyed the creation and running of my 2CV 620cc-engined Brooklands, I found the need to continue a building project too strong to resist, so encouraged and egged-on by Mike Meakin, the decision to do a Moto Guzzi conversion was taken. The first step was to source a suitable donor. eBay was the obvious choice, and it wasn't long before a suitable candidate appeared about 30 miles away. Bidding was successful and Mike and I trailered the 750cc SP home after each having a ride on it and enjoying its performance. Mileage showed at just over 10,000 which, given the performance, sounded about right. The appearance of the bike was spoiled by the corrosion all over the alloy components, otherwise it was in good order. Fired up with all the enthusiasm of a new project, I removed the engine/gearbox assembly from the frame, a straightforward procedure but one unique to the Guzzi.

"There followed a deal of heart searching brought on by friends comments of 'vandalism' at scrapping a potentially restorable machine, Mike not helping matters by expressing a desire to take on the bike's restoration if I would part with it.

"A chance browse on eBay revealed a 750cc Strada which had been the donor of an abandoned trike project. Here was the engine I wanted, with no recriminations of vandalism; that deed had already been done! A successful purchase saw Mike and I pick up my treasure, which, much to my surprise, included most of the original bike minus the frame, which had been chopped up to form the trike chassis. Now the project could start in earnest. More details of the build are under www.pembleton.co.uk.

"I am happy to report that as per April 2009, the Moto Guzzi-engined Brooklands passed its MoT, and is now up and running. Initial reactions are 'WOW,' it certainly does fly, and with a very healthy bark; I shall have to watch the loud peddle in town."

The Pembleton Brooklands with its 750cc Strada engine.

Hardtail Guzzi at the Chopper Club meeting, Buxton, May bank holiday 2009. (Courtesy Nicholas Stevens)

BLACKJACK TRIKES, HELSTON, CORNWALL
WWW.BLACKJACKZERO.COM

Blackjack is essentially a one-man business, run by Richard Oakes and supported by three or four sub-contractors. The company specialises in the design and manufacture of small numbers of high-quality roadster trikes.

Richard says: "The Zero delivers the excitement of a bike with greater comfort, more sociability and a reverse gear. Light and elemental, the Zero involves you with the driving experience, evoking the delights of vintage sports car motoring in a thoroughly contemporary way."

DEAN McMURRAY'S GUZZI, EAST SUSSEX

Dean's Guzzi story: "The original bike was a 1987 Guzzi Spada, in rough but running condition. Essentially, I liked the engine and handling, but not the aesthetics. With a limited budget I set out to rebuild it into something, at least to me, more pleasing to the eye. The bike is hard to classify. It's not a chopper, bobber, street fighter or rat, which I kind of like. It's just a custom that draws on a range of styles and influences, but remains minimalist, rideable, comfortable, relatively cheap to own, and a bit different.

"The bike uses the engine cradle from the original Guzzi Tonti frame, but with the footrest location and rear subframe modified.

"Forks are original Guzzi items mounted on alloy slab yokes. Handlebars were found in the shed.

"Cast wheels have been swapped for spoked items, and wider rims and tyres are fitted. The swinging arm was modified to allow the wider rear wheel/tyre to fit.

"The fuel tank is a Harley (FXR, I think) item modified to fit, warning light, digital speedo and fuel gauge are built into the centre console.

"The seat is a homemade base, clad in brown leather and stuffed with gel pads. Controls are a mixture of Harley, Japanese, and homemade. The left foot operates the clutch, and my left hand the gears.

"The engine has been breathed on by the previous owner and features hotter cams, bigger valves and carbs. It goes quite well. The transmission runs a jockey shift and suicide clutch converted by me.

"Exhausts are just bits of tube with a right angle bend and a small set of baffles to keep the neighbors a little happier.

"Wiring by me, and as much as possible, has been uprated by fitting Jap stuff and keeping it simple.

"A great big Harley battery and some of the electrics live in the leather side bag, which was originally designed to carry shotgun cartridges for pheasant hunting. This was arguably the most expensive part of the build. Paint-wise there isn't really any. I would have liked a bare metal finish but the English weather would not do it any favours, so everything that's not shiny has been powder-coated satin black.

The bike is hard to classify. Deano likes it this way. (Courtesy Sam McMurray)

"I've done all the construction bar the upholstery and powder-coating in a shed. When I'm not in the shed I work as a DT teacher in a local secondary school, and some of my students also helped in the stripping and fitting stages."

Left & above: A rare inline-mounted Guzzi-engined chopper photographed at the Custom Bike Show in Kent July 1991. (Courtesy Max from France)

Trikes are very popular in the UK. This California 1100 trike was photographed in December 2006 in Sandford Dorset, during the Mistletoe Run organized by the Dorset MC. (Courtesy Dan Jones)

Dave Osborne's BRA trike, (Courtesy Pete Morcombe)

Denis Brown's trike is based on a 2003 Guzzi Nevada Club. It has a
Reliant Robin back axle, but with Suzuki GSXR disc brakes.

Moto Guzzi THREE-SEATER TRIKE

Blue Davies bought this trike about four years ago on eBay. It was in a bit of a state, however its frame is a 'Desperate Dan' frame; a famous builder. Blue spent thousands on it over the years. A Moto Guzzi California Jackal engine, front end and wiring were used to rebuild the trike. The axle is from a Triumph, and its drum brakes were replaced with Ford Fiesta Mk3 discs and calipers. The stainless parts were made by his good friend Jack.

A close-up of the axle.

Top left: Blue Davies' three-seater trike.

Left: Blue in action.

The Rosso Mondello built by Gigamachine, Budapest. The bike competed in the AMD 2007 European Championship of Custom Bike Building in the Freestyle class. The frame is an HPU Gigamachine/Chopper frame (www.gigamachine.hu). (Courtesy *Born to be WILD* magazine, Hungary)

Spanish Ducati modifier Radical Ducati made this 2003 Moto Guzzi California 1100cc-based bike in 2010. The Madrid-based company is more known for its stunning sport customs, but it's good to sometimes try something different.

The bike has a new, two-into-one exhaust and Supertrapp silencers, as well as 2cm longer-than-standard Ohlins shocks. Its forks also received Hyperpro springs, and a Discacciati radial master cylinder helps in the braking department.

The Dirt Guzzi is a dirt track inspired version of a 2003 California 1100. (Courtesy www.radicalducati.com)

Ritmo Sereno is a Japanese company turning mainly European bikes such as BMWs and Moto Guzzis into beautiful café racers. The team sells parts and complete bikes made to order. The website (www. ritmo-sereno.com) is all in Japanese, but the gallery is still worth a look. The company put together the following very nice Guzzi Ambassador with modern brakes.

The 750cc bike features black Excel rims and 300mm AP floating disc brakes at the front. The brake and gear linkages are handmade. A lightened flywheel, Keihin CR carburettors and K&N air filters, a five-speed Le Mans gearbox and the custom stainless steel/aluminum exhaust complete the package. Lastly, the solo seat can be supplemented with a pillion pad within minutes.

The bike was prepared by Shiro Nakajima.

THE GUZZI BOARD TRACKER

Twenty-year-old Adam Nestor from southern Sweden is the creator of this blue board track Guzzi. Adam names his father as his main influence for his remarkable skills, helping Adam build his first bike when he was 16. Adam is now a qualified bike mechanic, and working full time with a motorcycle shop in Gothenburg. Expect to see more of this builder in the future!

Most of the parts for the board tracker were handmade by Adam, including the frame, fuel tank, velocity stacks, bars, exhaust, and lots of smaller, beautiful detailing. Only the seat was an outsourced item. The bike features Benelli hubs, Avon Speed Master tyres, Marzocchi forks, and an Ohlins rear shock. 'Madame Guzzi' won the best in show award at the 2010 Västervik bike show in Sweden.

Adam's 'Madame Guzzi.' (Courtesy Adam Nestor)

The board tracker has twin SU HS2 carburetors and an Ohlins shock absorber. (Courtesy Adam Nestor)

'Madame Guzzi' is based around a 1979 SP1000 engine. (Courtesy Adam Nestor)

CHAPTER 7

MOTO MORINI

Inspired by Mario Mazzetti, Alfonso Morini built a single-cylinder 125cc two-stroke racing bike as early as 1925. The design was so successful that Alfonso won six world records in 1927 in Monza under the Moto Morini name. Morini then began production of 350cc and 500cc three-wheelers in 1937 in Bologna, some of which had advanced features for the time, such as a shaft drive.

This 350cc model had a top speed of 70kph/44mph and a load capacity of 350kg. (Courtesy Giorgio Nada Editore)

The Motofurgone chassis ran on 4.00x17 Pirellis.

Nowadays probably best known for its 350cc and 500cc V-twin models of the 1970s, the company was bought by Cagiva in 1987, changed hands again in 1996 to Texas Pacific Group, and came again under Morini ownership in 1999. In 2004, the company launched a new range of 1200cc V-twins. The new engine was designed by Franco

Lambertini, the same engineer who penned the 350cc engine in the 1970s. The new Morinis were very nice bikes, but didn't sell enough in sufficient numbers and, sadly, Moto Morini went into liquidation in 2009.

The company produced its Excalibur cruiser in 350cc and 500cc guises from 1986 to 1993. The factory custom initially had cast wheels, but these were changed to wire wheels for the New York model from

Stefano Bellina's Excalibur.

Excalibur brochure from 1992.

1989-1991, after which the model reverted back to the Excalibur name. These smaller V-twins were capable cruisers, delivering 34hp for the 350cc and 42hp for the 500cc model.

The factory cruiser lent itself to customization, or, shall we say, 'Harleyfication,' owing to its V-twin engine configuration.

This custom with modified Morini frame has a Suzuki swingarm, Moto Guzzi rear fender, and Aprilia tank.

Phil Piper from www.choppershack.com also went down the Harley route in 1996 when building the New York, New York, Morini chopper below. The rare 501cc custom became an unusual and stunning multi-show winner.

Massi Apisto's custom job.

A 350cc-based Morini chopper, seen in 2001 at a vintage swap meet in Novegro near Milan. (Courtesy www.motalia.de)

Note the 80-spoke wheels and eight-pot rear brake setup.

The last of the Morini customs is Don Cronin's stand-out 'Medaza' chopper from Ireland.

Don, a sculptor and also a bike builder, sourced the engine for this project from a Morini Camel trail bike. Ger Conlon from C&C Choppers built the one-off frame, using an H-D Softail swingarm and pivot plates, relocating the shock mount from under the transmission to the top of the bike under the seat. The rear coil-over suspension comes from a Victory bike, while the front of the bike features a DNA Springer fork.

Don used his foundry skills to cast parts for the motor, like the clutch cover, cam cover and new rocker boxes. He then made a set of stainless steel exhausts and brass covers for the filters on the stock Dell'Orto carburetors.

He also built the dummy gas tank, which houses the bike's electrics, and the rear fender/taillight assembly. The actual gas tank is the brass pannier on the right side of the bike. Fuel is pumped from there to the carbs by an SU fuel pump from an original Mini car. A front Morini Strada hub was built into an eBay-sourced rim, while the back rim was built using a Morini Enduro hub. Both front and rear brakes are original Morini drums.

Pictures courtesy of Horst Roesler and Frank Sander, and AMD World Championships (www.amdchampionship.com).

The gas tank is the brass pannier on the right side of the bike.

Don cast the clutch cover, cam cover and new rocker boxes in his foundry.

The front end features DNA springs.

The 'Medaza' was an entry in the 2009 World Championship of Custom Bike Building – Freestyle category.

BMW CUSTOM MOTORCYCLES

Choppers, Cruisers, Bobbers, Trikes & Quads

ISBN: 978-1-845843-25-0
Hardback • 25x25cm • £19.99* UK/$39.95* USA
128 pages • 270 colour and b&w pictures

JAPANESE CUSTOM MOTORCYCLES

The Nippon Chop – Chopper, Cruiser, Bobber, Trikes and Quads

Uli Cloesen

ISBN: 978-1-845845-30-8
Hardback • 25x25cm • £25* UK/$39.95* USA
128 pages • 275 colour pictures

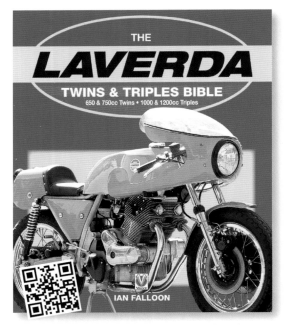

ISBN: 978-1-845840-58-7 Hardback
25x20.7cm • £29.99* UK/$59.95* USA
160 pages • 222 colour and b&w pictures

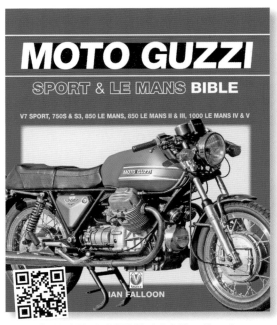

ISBN: 978-1-845840-64-8 Hardback
25x20.7cm • £29.99* UK/$59.95* USA
160 pages • 160 colour and b&w pictures

ISBN: 978-1-845843-21-2 Hardback
25x20.7cm • £30.00* UK/$59.95* USA
160 pages • 197 colour pictures

ISBN: 978-1-84584-121-8 Hardback
25x20.7cm • £29.99* UK/$59.95* USA
160 pages • 178 colour and b&w pictures

ISBN: 978-1-84584-202-4 Hardback
25x25cm • £40.00* UK/$79.95* USA
176 pages • 259 colour and b&w pictures

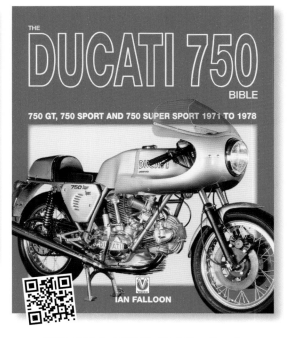

ISBN: 978-1-845840-12-9 Hardback
25x20.7cm • £29.99* UK/$59.95* USA
160 pages • 163 colour and b&w pictures

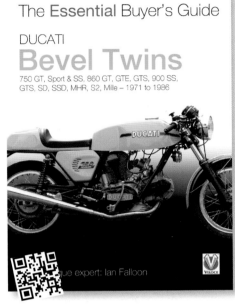

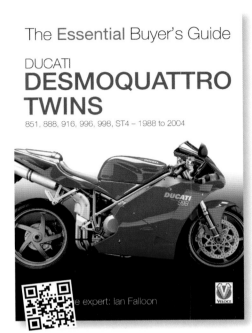

INDEX